Bylines

A Photobiography of Nellie Bly

{Bylines}

A Photobiography of Nellie Bly

Sue Macy

FOREWORD BY LINDA ELLERBEE

NATIONAL GEOGRAPHIC
WASHINGTON, D.C.

In memory of Maggie Stevaralgia and Lucy Evankow

PUBLISHED BY THE NATIONAL GEOGRAPHIC SOCIETY
John M. Fahey, Jr., *President and Chief Executive Officer*
Gilbert M. Grosvenor, *Chairman of the Board*
Tim T. Kelly, *President, Global Media Group*
John Q. Griffin, *President, Publishing*
Nina D. Hoffman, *Executive Vice President; President, Book Publishing Group*

PREPARED BY THE BOOK DIVISION
Nancy Laties Feresten, *Vice President, Editor in Chief, Children's Books*
Bea Jackson, *Director of Design and Illustrations, Children's Books*
Amy Shields, *Executive Editor, Series, Children's Books*
Jennifer Emmett, *Executive Editor, Reference and Solo, Children's Books*
Carl Mehler, *Director of Maps*

STAFF FOR THIS BOOK
Jennifer Emmett, *Editor*
Lori Epstein, *Illustrations Editor*
Marty Ittner, *Designer*
Matt Chwastyk, *Map Production*
Connie D. Binder, *Indexer*
Lewis Bassford, *Production Project Manager*
Jennifer A. Thornton, *Managing Editor*
Grace Hill, *Associate Managing Editor*
R. Gary Colbert, *Production Director*
Susan Borke, *Legal and Business Affairs*

MANUFACTURING AND QUALITY MANAGEMENT
Christopher A. Liedel, *Chief Financial Officer*
Phillip L. Schlosser, *Vice President*
Chris Brown, *Technical Director*
Nicole Elliott, *Manager*

The body text of the book is set in Minion Pro.
The display text is Knockout, and the quotes are set in Matrix Script.

Printed in China

LIBRARY OF CONGRESS CATALOGING-IN-PUBLICATION DATA
Macy, Sue.
   Bylines : a photobiography of Nellie Bly / by Sue Macy.
      p. cm.
   Includes bibliographical references and index.
   ISBN 978-1-4263-0513-9 (hardcover : alk. paper) — ISBN 978-1-4263-0514-6 (library binding : alk. paper)
   1. Bly, Nellie, 1864-1922—Pictorial works—Juvenile literature.
   2. Women journalists—United States—Biography—Pictorial works—Juvenile literature. I. Title.
   PN4874.C59M33 2009
   070.92—dc22
   [B]   2008052329

COVER: This is one of several photographic portraits that were taken of Nellie before and after her trip around the world in 1889-1890. She was 25 years old at the time.

BACK COVER: McLoughlin Brothers issued the first *Round the World with Nellie Bly* board game in 1890. Over the years new editions were printed and the art on the box was updated. One later version showed an airplane in the background, even though Nellie circled the globe 14 years before the Wright brothers made their first successful flight.

TITLE PAGE: Another portrait of Nellie as a young globetrotter is superimposed on her byline from one of her fiction stories published in the *New York Family Story Paper* in 1894. The same background appears on page one.

OPPOSITE: Nellie sat for this portrait early in the 20th century, when she was about 40 years old.

ACKNOWLEDGEMENTS
Anyone who writes about Nellie Bly owes a huge debt to Brooke Kroeger, author of the superb book *Nellie Bly: Daredevil, Reporter, Feminist*. I thank her for creating such a fantastic, authoritative resource. Thanks, too, to the staffs at the libraries where I did the bulk of my research, including the Library of Congress, Princeton's Firestone Library, Carnegie Library of Pittsburgh, Doe Library at the University of California at Berkeley, and the Apollo Memorial Library in Apollo, Pennsylvania.

I also appreciate the support and patience of my talented friends at National Geographic, starting with Jennifer Emmett, who's had at least two babies since I began this book. It's always a pleasure to work with her, as well as inspired designer Marty Ittner, master photo editor Lori Epstein, editor-in-chief extraordinaire Nancy Feresten, and the rest of the Children's Books staff.

Finally, I thank my friends and family, who followed the progress of this book with eager anticipation, always asking how "Nellie" was doing. Those supporters include my parents and brother, as well as Sheila Wolinsky, the late Fran Janssen, and Jackie Glasthal. This book is dedicated to the memory of Maggie Stevaralgia and Lucy Evankow, former colleagues and stalwarts of Scholastic's library, who were as much a part of New York in their day as Nellie Bly was in hers.

"Energy rightly applied and directed will accomplish anything."

Foreword

I'm a journalist who, for the last 18 years, has tried to explain the events of the world to young people on a television series called *Nick News*. But I've never tried to explain myself on our show. Maybe I should have. Why did I become a journalist? What does a journalist do? Just how do you get that story? And what was (is) it like to be a female in what, for years, was pretty much an all-male profession?

I know what it was like for me, even in the early 1970s, when I was a young journalist just starting out. It was hard. Most men still didn't like the idea of "girl reporters." And yet I also know it would have been much harder if I hadn't been able to stand on the shoulders of a few remarkable women who blazed a trail for me, and for other girls who came before and after me.

This is the story of one of those pioneers. Remember, not all pioneers wore coonskin caps and carried rifles. Some wore sunbonnets and carried babies. This one wore lace collars and carried a notebook. Her name was Nellie Bly. She was a journalist.

Born before the Civil War ended, this shy little girl grew up to become a world-class reporter at a time when females were supposed to stay home and, well, keep their mouths shut. Nellie wasn't good at either. She traveled, she reported, and she cared. She got involved. She had adventures. She made noise. She wanted to use journalism to change people's lives. And once in a while, this particular storyteller became the story.

You're going to like the story of Nellie Bly. It's real. It's true. It's exciting. And if this story is about Nellie, it's also about journalism, which I happen to think is one of the best jobs anyone can have. As a child, I was always warned not to talk to

Linda Ellerbee (center) floats in zero gravity with four kids who live much of their lives in wheelchairs in "The View from My Chair," an episode of *Nick News with Linda Ellerbee,* broadcast on Nickelodeon in 2008. The other adults are coaches, there to make sure no one gets hurt.

strangers, but, like Nellie, I've made a good living and had a wonderful life talking to strangers. Of course I've learned that after you talk to them, they're no longer strangers. And just imagine: As a journalist, they pay you to learn things. They pay you to meet the world's most interesting people, some of whom may live next door to you. They pay you to go to faraway places, to wade into the lives of people who are completely different from you, and then to tell everyone else what you've found out. And sometimes that does change the world.

Nellie once said, "I have never written a word that didn't come from my heart. I never shall." Very well. The following words come from my heart: I owe a lot to Nellie Bly.

All of us "girl reporters" do.   —*Linda Ellerbee*

Nellie Bly traveled to the most exotic cities on the globe by the time she was 25, but she started her life in a tiny village that was named after her father. Nellie, whose real name was Elizabeth Jane Cochran, was born May 5, 1864, in Cochran's Mills, Pennsylvania. Her father Michael was the son of Irish settlers who had come to western Pennsylvania in the early 19th century. He grew up to be a local politician and judge and made money buying and selling land. He also opened a general store and ran a gristmill for grinding grain in an area called Pitts' Mills. In 1855, his neighbors celebrated Cochran's contributions by renaming Pitts' Mills in his honor.

Michael Cochran already had 12 children by the time Elizabeth Jane was born. His first wife, the mother of ten, had died in 1857, and he had remarried a year later. Cochran's second wife, Mary Jane, gave birth to two sons before Elizabeth Jane and a daughter afterward. Fortunately, the family had lots of room in their two-story home on Crooked Creek.

Although the Civil War was still in progress in 1864, life went on undisturbed in Cochran's Mills. Farmers raised corn, oats, buckwheat, and rye. Miners removed salt, limestone, coal, and iron ore from the ground. The growing community soon had a doctor, a dentist, a school, and a post office, as well as several small businesses. By 1869, close to 200 families made this village in the hills of western Pennsylvania their home.

Michael Cochran's house in Cochran's Mills (inset) was taken down in the 1930s, and the land on which it stood was flooded during the building of the Crooked Creek Dam. This gristmill (background) in Blair County, Pennsylvania, about 80 miles away, is similar to the one in Cochran's Mills.

Rare portraits of Nellie's dad, Judge Michael Cochran, and mom, Mary Jane Kennedy Cochran, are shown against a panoramic photograph of Apollo, Pennsylvania, that continues on pages 12 and 13.

Thanks to her mother, Elizabeth Jane Cochran stood out from everyone else. Elizabeth was Mary Jane's first daughter—not including her five stepdaughters—and her mother refused to dress her in the dull grays and browns worn by most children in town. Instead, Elizabeth Jane wore pink. The color became her favorite, and then it became her nickname. Elizabeth would call herself Pink or Pinkey Cochran throughout her younger years.

When Pink was five years old, her father sold some land and used the money to build a luxurious new home in the nearby town of Apollo. All of the children from Michael Cochran's first marriage were old enough to live on their own, so only Pink, her three youngest siblings, and her parents moved in. The family also brought their cow, their horse, and their two dogs. The animals had a large yard to run around in, with plenty of grass for the cow and horse to eat.

With a population of 764 in 1870,

Nellie's first home in Apollo was still standing in the 21st century. In 2005 the house, now subdivided into four separate apartments, was sold to a new owner.

Apollo had almost twice as many residents as Cochran's Mills and more businesses and craftspeople. Pink's father had grown up there, and he returned to enjoy his success in familiar surroundings. The family continued to grow with the birth of Pink's youngest brother, Harry. But the Cochrans' carefree life in their new mansion was short-lived. Early in the summer of 1870, Michael Cochran became ill, and on July 19, he died. Pink was just six years old. Harry was a four-month-old infant.

Michael's death left his family stunned and saddened. Beyond their grief, however, were practical concerns about the future. Despite his experience in the legal field, Michael Cochran did not leave a will stating what should be done with his money and property. His older children went to court to ask a judge to determine how to divide their father's estate.

Close to 140 years after Michael Cochran's death, his pocket-watch remained a prized possession of Linda H. Champanier, a descendant of Michael's eldest son.

"It is a strange fact that the further one goes from home the more loyal one becomes."

Just 25 miles from Pittsburgh, Apollo lies on the Kiskiminetas River, a tributary of the Allegheny. This 1909 panoramic view shows the community during a period of growth. The 1910 census reported 3,006 citizens in Apollo, close to four times the number that was there when Nellie and her family moved to town.

Apollo, Pa. by A.W. Moore, Va...

One of Michael's older sons, William Worth Cochran, had died while serving as a Union soldier in the Civil War. The judge ruled that each of the 14 surviving children deserved an equal share of his or her father's assets. The younger children's money would be kept for them until they were adults. Mary Jane also would get a regular income to help raise her five small children. In order to figure out how much money each family member should receive, their father's property would have to be sold. That included his land in and around Cochran's Mills, as well as the Cochrans' beautiful new home.

Within a few months, Pink's mother bought a more modest house nearby and moved her family into it. Once the financial issues stemming from Michael Cochran's death were settled, Mary Jane started receiving about $16 per week to run her household. That was a decent income in the 1870s—more than a factory worker earned—but it was far less than what the Cochrans were used to. Even so, Mary Jane did her best to ensure that her children led happy, comfortable lives. She paid for piano and organ lessons for Pink and encouraged her to keep up with her horseback riding, which she loved.

Two and a half years after she lost her husband, Mary Jane Cochran married John Jackson (Jack) Ford, a Civil War veteran whose wife had died six months earlier. Ford had led an adventurous life, even going west to join the Gold Rush in the 1850s. But he hadn't found much success. His new family quickly learned that he had a bad temper, particularly when he drank. Ford threatened and sometimes hit his wife, flying into rages at home and in public. Mary Jane's hopes for security and companionship gave way to a life of constant fear. After five years of suffering, she left Ford and filed for divorce. Pink and her oldest brother

Nellie's half brother, William Worth Cochran, died on January 6, 1864, four months before she was born. He served with the 103rd Regiment, a unit of volunteer soldiers from Pennsylvania like the ones shown here.

Albert testified at the divorce proceedings. "Ford has been generally drunk since they were married," said 14-year-old Pink. "When drunk, he is very cross. . . . Ford threatened to do mother harm. Mother was afraid of him."

By the time Mary Jane's divorce was final, Pink was 15 years old. She was determined to find a way to earn a living so that she and her mother did not have to depend on men like Jack Ford. Pink decided to become a teacher. In September 1879, she entered a three-year program at the State Normal School in Indiana, Pennsylvania (now Indiana University of Pennsylvania). This private school was one of 12 in the state dedicated to training young men and women for careers in education or business. One of the first things Pink did at the Normal School was give up her nickname. Instead of Pink Cochran she became Elizabeth J. Cochrane, with an "e" at the end of

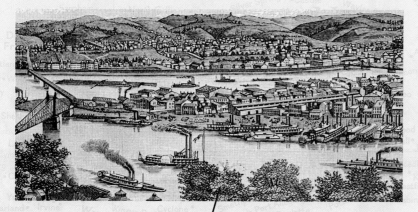

Pittsburgh would become known as "The City of Bridges" because of the number of spans built to cross the three rivers that run through it. There are at least two bridges in this 1887 engraving and many more today. The picture shows the Allegheny (top) and the Monongahela (bottom) joining to form the Ohio (left).

When Nellie entered the State Normal School in Indiana, Pennsylvania, it was a new institution, having opened its doors for the first time in 1875. It became Indiana University of Pennsylvania in 1965 and today boasts an enrollment of more than 14,000 students in its undergraduate and graduate programs.

her last name to make it more distinguished. Eventually, her brothers and even her mother would adopt this new spelling of their family name.

At school, Elizabeth studied grammar, reading, writing, arithmetic, drawing, and spelling. She seemed excited as she described her experiences in letters home, but that excitement quickly turned to disappointment. Toward the end of her first term, Elizabeth learned that she would have to leave school. The problem was money. She had planned to cover her tuition and expenses—a total of about $200 per year—with the funds that had been put away for her after her father died. The banker who was overseeing her account had told her she had enough money for three years of school. In fact, after only half a year, all of her money was gone. Elizabeth later would sue the banker for misusing her funds, though the suit dragged on and she eventually dropped it.

Meanwhile, Elizabeth was so upset that she returned to Apollo instead of taking her exams and finishing the term. But she did not remain there long. Her brother Charles had moved to the nearby city of Pittsburgh to earn a living, and her brother Albert had joined him soon afterward. By the end of 1880, Mary Jane followed them with Elizabeth and her two youngest children, Kate and Harry.

Pittsburgh had a population of 156,389 in 1880, making it the 12th largest city in the United States. Located at the point where the Allegheny and the Monongahela rivers join to form the Ohio, it was a manufacturing and shipping hub. The landscape was crowded with smokestacks and church towers, and the streets were crowded with people. After the Civil War ended in 1865, thousands of immigrants had flocked to the Iron City to work in its iron and steel mills.

Mary Jane and her family settled in Allegheny City, a suburb just north of

Pittsburgh that was home to an additional 78,682 people. Elizabeth's older brothers worked at a series of jobs and eventually got married. Kate married, too, at age 16, and one year later she gave birth to a baby girl. Mary Jane took in boarders to make ends meet, and it is likely that Elizabeth found work as a nanny and a tutor. But little is known about how she spent her time in Pittsburgh until 1885.

In January of that year, Elizabeth read a series of columns in a newspaper that changed her life. The columns were written by Erasmus Wilson, who regularly shared his views as the "Quiet Observer" on the staff of the *Pittsburg Dispatch*. Wilson's subject was the role of women in society, and his opinion was that women should stay out of the workplace and instead focus on cooking, cleaning, sewing, and keeping a nice home. A woman's mission in life, Wilson said, was to be a helpmate to a man, not to compete with him.

Wilson's "quiet observations" did not sit well with Elizabeth. She only had to think of her mother to know that women could not always depend on men. Elizabeth grew angry at Wilson's assumption that every woman could find all that she needed through marriage. She expressed her opinions in a letter to the newspaper's editor, George Madden. The letter, signed "Lonely Orphan Girl," did not include Elizabeth's name or home address. But Madden was so intrigued by her passionate arguments that he included the following notice in the January 17, 1885, edition of the *Dispatch*: "If the writer of the communication signed 'Lonely Orphan Girl' will send her name and address to this office, merely as a guarantee of good faith, she will confer a favor and receive the information she desires."

Rather than sending in her name and address, Elizabeth showed up at the newspaper's office herself. Erasmus Wilson later wrote about the arrival of this

Despite the difference of opinion that brought them together, Nellie and Erasmus Wilson would develop a lifelong friendship. Her letters to him over the years remain a rare source of insight into Nellie's innermost feelings about her life and work.

"shy little girl," who was out of breath after climbing the four flights of stairs to the newsroom. She seemed terrified, Wilson recalled, until she met Madden. The editor was young and friendly and immediately put Elizabeth at ease. After discussing her concerns, he suggested that she write her own article for the *Dispatch* on "the woman's sphere." It was Elizabeth's first official newspaper assignment and she threw herself into it with great enthusiasm.

Readers of the January 25, 1885, edition of the *Pittsburg Dispatch* found Elizabeth's first published words on page 11. Her article carried the headline "The Girl Puzzle" and the byline "Orphan Girl." In the compelling, compassionate style that would become her trademark, she urged her readers to consider the plight of widows and unmarried girls who were not blessed with great beauty, talent, or wealth. These women needed the opportunity to earn a living, she insisted, but current attitudes restricted the types of jobs available to them. "Let a youth start as errand boy and he will work his way up until he is one of the firm," she wrote. "Girls are just as smart, a great deal quicker to learn; why, then, can they not do the same?" Women should be hired as bank tellers, train conductors, and traveling salespeople, she argued, and they should be paid the same wages as men. If that were the case, she concluded, "Their lives would be brighter, their health better, their pocketbooks fuller."

George Madden saw promise in Elizabeth's work and asked her to write another article right away. She chose divorce as her subject, filling almost two columns of the February 1, 1885, *Dispatch* with her thoughts on how a couple

Photographs of women working in factories in the 1880s are rare. Nellie's series on Pittsburgh's "factory girls" was accompanied by drawings. These women are making shoes in a Massachusetts factory a little later, around 1895.

could avoid divorce by having honest discussions before they were married. This article gave the public their first glimpse of a byline that would become familiar around the world: *Nellie Bly*. In the 1880s, female newspaper reporters rarely signed their own names to their work. They used pseudonyms. As George Madden rushed Elizabeth's article into print, he asked his staff to suggest a pseudonym for the "Orphan Girl." Someone called out "Nelly Bly," the title of a popular song written 35 years earlier by Pittsburgh native Stephen Collins Foster. The Nelly Bly in the song was the daughter of a former slave who worked as a servant in the home of Foster's friend. George Madden liked the name and added it to the end of Elizabeth's article, misspelling "Nelly" by mistake. It turned out to be an appropriate byline. The reporter Nellie Bly would spend a good deal of her career writing about the lives of poor women like the Nelly in the song.

In fact, Pittsburgh's newest woman reporter suggested a series about the city's female factory workers as her next assignment. Madden liked the idea, and he also liked Nellie. He offered her a permanent job at the *Dispatch* at a salary of $5 per week. Her first article as a staff reporter, in the February 8 edition, chronicled the social lives of Pittsburgh's poor working women. In the weeks that followed, Nellie took a close look at eight Pittsburgh factories where women helped to produce everything from barbed wire to cigars. Her articles shed light on the anonymous women who toiled 12 or more hours a day for an average daily pay of $1. "At first I was very much ashamed to be a factory girl," one wire worker told her. "I had always been told factory girls were the worst girls on earth, but I have found some very nice, sensible ones here. . . . I have learned a girl can be a lady as well in a factory as in a parlor."

"Can they that have full and plenty of the world's goods realize what it is to be a poor working woman, abiding in one or two bare rooms, without fire enough to keep warm?"

Nellie's eight-part series did much to humanize Pittsburgh's female factory workers for her readers. "There are some people who think factory workers are horrible," she said to one of the women. "Well, they are as good as the ones that look down on them," the worker answered. The women shown here are packing syrup and cooked fruit into glass jars at a bottling plant around 1890.

Nellie's factory girls series proved she could tackle gritty topics, but her next articles were decidedly more lightweight. Madden assigned her to the areas frequently covered by women: gardening, social news, arts and entertainment, and fashion. Nellie reported on the annual flower show, surveyed the latest fashions in shoes, dresses, and hairstyles, and profiled a woman who ran an opera company. In September she started writing a regular column in which she shared her observations and insights about life in Pittsburgh. She used the column to take up the cause of the city's working women once again, calling for charitable organizations to set up a safe place for poor women to spend their free time. One reader was so touched by Nellie's plea that she wrote, "If we had more people like Nellie Bly to think of something for the good of the working girl, it would be better for us."

While she enjoyed the praise, Nellie was growing tired of writing articles about flowers and hair care. Before the end of 1885, she left the staff of the paper and began submitting stories on a freelance basis. Nellie was 21 years old and ready for adventure. As a *Dispatch* reporter, she had met a group of visitors from Mexico who had invited her to travel in their country. Realizing that most Americans knew little about the nation to their south, Nellie decided to become a foreign correspondent and send back reports about this mysterious land. Although George Madden tried to talk her out of her plans, he agreed to publish the articles. Early in 1886, she packed her bags and took the four-day train trip to the Mexican border. Her mother came along as chaperone because it wasn't seen as proper for a young woman to travel alone.

Nellie spoke no Spanish, but she found enough English-speaking sources to be able to report on a wide array of subjects. From a home base in the "City

These pictures, taken by photographer William Henry Jackson, show Mexico in the same year that Nellie visited. In her articles, Nellie made a point of describing what she saw in great detail, from the food to the street markets (right) to the people she met on her trips around the country.

of Mexico" (Mexico City), she and her mother took train trips around the countryside. On one such trip, they astonished their fellow travelers by carrying their own bags. "I defied their gaze," wrote Nellie, "and showed them that a free American girl can accommodate herself to circumstances without the aid of a man." But Nellie's independent spirit got her into trouble. In mid-March, she

No. 1324.   20 Cents.

In 1889, Nellie's articles about Mexico were collected in book form (background). Though she praised President Porfirio Díaz (right) in her initial reports, she was highly critical of him and his government in the pieces she wrote after returning to Pittsburgh.

No. 1324.   Annual Subscription $30.   Entered at the Post Office, New York, as second class matter, Jan. 3, 1889.

"The Mexican papers never publish one word against the government or officials and the people who are at their mercy dare not breathe one word against them, as those in position are more able than the most tyrannical czar to make their lives miserable."

SIX MONTHS IN MEXICO

BY

NELLIE BLY,

AUTHOR OF "TEN DAYS IN A MAD HOUSE," &C.

sent the *Dispatch* an article about a local editor who was arrested for writing editorials that criticized Mexico's government. She explained that the government regularly forced editors to keep controversial articles out of their newspapers. Nellie's *Dispatch* piece eventually made its way to Mexican officials, and they threatened to arrest her for defying their censorship laws. The threats made Nellie nervous enough to end her Mexican adventure. In mid-June, she and her mother returned to Pittsburgh.

Even after she was home, Nellie continued to write about Mexico. She admitted that while she was away, she had chosen the topics of her articles carefully to avoid being jailed. Now she wrote more freely. Nellie criticized Mexican president Porfirio Díaz and called his government "the worst monarchy in existence." For nearly three months, she shared vivid tales of Mexican censorship and corruption. When she ran out of material, she rejoined the staff of the *Dispatch*, this time as an arts and theater reporter. But Nellie soon grew restless. Covering the local arts scene could not compare to the excitement of being a foreign correspondent. Without consulting anyone at the newspaper, she made her next career move. In the spring of 1887, Nellie Bly headed east to work in the most thrilling newspaper town of all—New York.

Nellie hardly took New York by storm. In fact, she used up nearly all of her savings as she looked for a job on one of the city's newspapers. Finally, she convinced George Madden to buy some features for the *Dispatch* on women's fashions and other aspects of life in New York. Madden couldn't pass up the chance to have Nellie's spirited writing back in the paper, even if she had left him in the lurch. It was a good thing, too, because the money from those freelance articles allowed Nellie to continue renting a small, furnished room on the Upper West Side of Manhattan. The articles also led to a breakthrough. In August, she reported that she had received a letter from "a lady, ambitious and presumably young," asking if New York was the best place for a woman to begin a career in journalism. Nellie promptly set up interviews with the editors of the top papers in the city and then reported their answers in the *Dispatch*. It was a brilliant career move. Besides collecting material for the story, the interviews helped Nellie get her foot in the door in her own job search.

Not that the editors were encouraging. Charles A. Dana of the *Sun* told Nellie that he thought men reported stories more accurately than women because women found it "impossible not to exaggerate." Dr. George H. Hepworth of the *Herald* said it was improper for a woman to cover a story about a crime or a scandal, so he would only assign such a story to a man. He added that having women in the office made men uncomfortable. "The men do not feel at liberty to take off their coats or rest their feet on the desks," he said, nor could they "give vent to their feelings in the language all grades of angry men employ." Colonel John A. Cockerill of the *World* agreed that he would assign women only certain types of stories, such as features on fashion and society events. "What they are fitted for is so limited," he said, "that a man is of far greater service" as a reporter.

Nellie's article was published in the *Dispatch* on August 21, 1887, and newspapers in other cities printed excerpts in the weeks that followed. Each time a paper picked up the story, Nellie's reputation grew. She used this success to set up a meeting with Colonel Cockerill at the *World* to talk about her own

When Nellie joined the staff of the *New York World,* the paper's publisher, Joseph Pulitzer, had plans to build a new headquarters. Rising 309 feet, the New York World Building (center), also called the Pulitzer Building, was the tallest skyscraper in the world when it was completed on December 10, 1890. It was torn down in 1955 to extend the entrance ramp for the Brooklyn Bridge.

Joseph Pulitzer immigrated from Hungary at age 17 and became a giant in American journalism.

career. Despite his views on the limited value of female reporters, Cockerill liked Nellie's story ideas and wanted to hire her. He gave her $25 up front and asked her to come back after he had a chance to consult with Joseph Pulitzer, the paper's publisher. The money could not have come at a better time. Nellie was broke. She had borrowed carfare from her landlady just to get to the *World*'s offices.

Cockerill had told Nellie that women were cut out to cover only the more refined news stories. But the first assignment he gave her was daunting, even dangerous. It was an early example of stunt journalism, in which a reporter becomes part of the story by going undercover or writing about her own experiences in a challenging situation. In this case, Cockerill hired Nellie to investigate alleged abuses at the Women's Lunatic Asylum on Blackwell's Island in New York. The asylum housed women who were committed after being declared insane by doctors or a judge. To do the job right, Nellie had to be committed there herself. If she had any misgivings about the task, they were outweighed by her determination to succeed. Looking back at the experience several months later, she wrote, "I never in my life turned back from a course I had started upon."

First, Nellie had to establish a new identity. One morning, she put on old clothes and wandered down Second Avenue to Matron Irene Stenard's Temporary Home for Females. She rented a room at this women's shelter

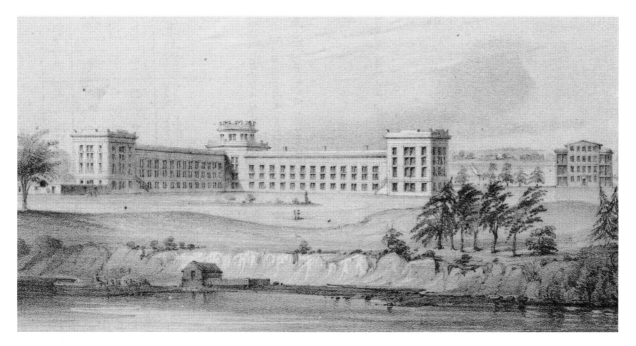

Blackwell's Island housed a number of buildings in 1887. Besides the Lunatic Asylum (shown here), at the north end of the island, the island had a charity hospital, a prison, and an almshouse (a poorhouse, for needy or homeless people).

for 30 cents a night, registering as Nellie Brown and doing her best to keep a startled look on her face. She refused to sleep and told anyone who spoke to her that the trunks containing her belongings had disappeared. She also complained of a headache that made her forget things. In the morning, a woman from Matron Stenard's took Nellie to the Essex County Police Court, where a kindly judge determined that she had been drugged and left wandering about New York. He sent her to be examined at Bellevue Hospital. There, she told a doctor that she was from the island of Cuba and acted confused as he asked her a battery of questions. The doctor finally pronounced her "positively demented." He told a nurse, "I consider it a hopeless case. She needs to be put where someone will take care of her." After two nights at Bellevue, Nellie was taken by boat across the East River to Blackwell's Island.

"I began to have a smaller regard for the ability of doctors than I had ever had before. I felt sure now that no doctor could tell whether people were insane or not."

Art depicting the female inmates of the Lunatic Asylum on Blackwell's Island often was overly dramatic. This engraving appeared in a publication in 1898.

IN THE HANDS OF THE POLICE.

HER BEDROOM.

Nellie's reports on her "10 days in a madhouse" (background) included illustrations by *World* cartoonist Walt McDougall, who accompanied the newspaper's lawyer to obtain her release from Blackwell's Island.

During the next ten days, Nellie got a firsthand look at the deplorable living conditions in the Women's Asylum. She later captured every detail for the readers of the *World*. "The Insane Asylum on Blackwell's Island is a human rat-trap," she wrote. She described the numbing cold of the hallways and sleeping quarters and the inadequate clothing inmates were forced to wear. She told of the skimpy meals and tasteless food, including bread with butter that was "so horrible that one could not eat it" and "a chunk of beef, which, on investigation, proved to be slightly spoiled." She remembered baths, given only once a week, in which one woman after another would bathe in the same tub of water until it was black with filth. And she chronicled the actions of the cruel nurses who constantly reminded the inmates, "This is charity, and you should be thankful for what you get."

Nellie described inmates who had been sent to Blackwell's Island because they were poor or weakened by illness. She wrote about foreign-born women who could not convince doctors of their sanity because they did not speak English. "I determined then and there," she wrote, "that I would try by every means to make my mission a benefit to my suffering sisters." After the newspaper sent a lawyer to secure her release, Nellie's two-part account of her experiences dominated the front pages of the *World*. The October 9 and October 16, 1887, editions featured a total of 17 tightly packed columns of her detailed and heart-wrenching prose. Other newspapers quickly spread the word, in New York and across North America. The plight of her "suffering sisters" no longer could be ignored.

Improvements were made almost immediately at Blackwell's Island. When Nellie returned there with a group of investigators in late October, she found better food and more sanitary conditions. She also learned that the foreign patients she had written about had been moved out of the Women's Asylum. Meanwhile, New York's leaders voted to increase the annual budget for hospitals and prisons, with at least $50,000 more promised to the asylum at Blackwell's Island. Nellie's own finances improved as well, since her exposé earned her a full-time job on the *World*. She quickly got to work on other stunt assignments. She posed as a maid for a story on how employment agencies treated job seekers. She passed herself off as an unwed mother for an article on people who sold unwanted babies. And in a break from such serious material, she wrote about her experiences taking ballet lessons.

By making herself part of the story, Nellie developed an ever-growing base of loyal readers who bought the *World* to keep up with her exploits. In 1888, they followed as she went undercover to expose a fake hypnotist and a lobby-ist who bribed state officials to get bills passed or killed. They also witnessed Nellie's visits to police court to talk to female prisoners and her attempt to flush out a kidnapper in New York's Central Park. "Nothing was too strenuous nor too perilous for her if it promised results," remembered Walt McDougall, a cartoonist at the *World* who often illustrated Nellie's articles. "In sooth, she was more than once held back from a too dangerous venture."

Yet in 1889, there was no holding Nellie back from the most fantastic stunt of all. She proposed to circle the globe faster than the fictional character Phileas Fogg did in the 1873 novel by Jules Verne, *Around the World in Eighty Days*. It was an idea that the editors at the *World* already had been considering, but they were wary of sending a female reporter. A woman would need a chaperone, warned business manager George Turner, and she would likely require so much luggage that it would slow her down. Nellie said she would travel alone and she would bring only what she could carry. She also declared that if the *World* didn't give her the assignment, she would take the idea to one of New York's other newspapers. Colonel Cockerill quickly reassured Nellie that she would be the *World*'s globetrotter, and on Monday, November 11, 1889, he made it official. She would leave in only three days.

First thing Tuesday morning, Nellie headed to Ghormley's, a dressmaker on Fifth Avenue, where she ordered a travel gown in blue plaid fabric to be made by the end of the day. Elsewhere, she bought a lighter dress, a heavy plaid overcoat, a light raincoat, and a hat. She also bought two satchels, one about ten inches long by seven inches wide, and the other even smaller. In these Nellie packed everything she would bring on the trip: her dresses, undergarments, handkerchiefs, a pair of slippers, needles and thread, and other pieces of clothing and personal items, as well as pens, pencils, an inkstand, and paper. Although some people advised her to carry a gun for protection, she refused.

Nellie left Hoboken, New Jersey, for Southampton, England, aboard the ocean liner *Augusta Victoria* at 9:40 a.m. on Thursday, November 14. During her journey she would travel as a passenger on water and land, aiming to return home by January 27, just 75 days later. "The significance of the trip is not its scientific aspect," reported the *World* on November 14, "for it is hardly to be expected that Miss Bly will come back with any new theory of the

People all over the world came to know Nellie from this 1889 image. She is dressed in her plaid overcoat, carrying her travel bag and waving goodbye.

universe." However, the paper continued, "Her trip when ended will be a record of how far in this last quarter of the century the facilities for travel and communication have advanced."

Although Nellie didn't know it when she departed, she was not alone in her race around the world. The morning her journey began, John Brisben Walker, publisher of *Cosmopolitan* magazine, decided to send his own reporter to try and beat her. Elizabeth Bisland learned of her assignment only six hours before she boarded a train for San Francisco with a hastily packed steamer trunk for the first leg of her trip. She would take a westward route while Nellie traveled east. But the *World* played down the challenge from Bisland, hardly mentioning her in its pages. As for Nellie, she first learned she had a rival when she reached Hong

In 1891, Elizabeth Bisland (left) published *In Seven Stages: A Flying Trip Around the World,* a book about her own globetrotting journey. Bisland's chronicle of her hastily planned trip, made in a total of 76 days, is full of colorful descriptions and offers an interesting counterpoint to Nellie's.

Nellie left Hoboken, New Jersey, on the *Augusta Victoria* (top), a steamer owned by a German shipping company, the Hamburg-American Line. Once in Europe, she took a detour to meet Jules Verne (right), author of the book that inspired her journey.

Kong, 39 days into her adventure. "I am not racing with anyone," she said. She added that her goal was to make it home in 75 days, and the attempt of another globetrotter was not her concern.

Indeed, the biggest challenge in Nellie's quest to circle the globe quickly seemed to be making connections from one leg of the trip to the next. Missing a train or a ship could leave her stranded for as long as a week till the next one arrived. Even so, after the voyage on the *Augusta Victoria*, Nellie took a detour to meet Jules Verne, creator of the fictitious character whose record she was trying to beat. She traveled by ship across the English Channel to France and caught a train to Verne's home of Amiens for a brief audience with the famous author. After a detailed discussion of Nellie's travel route, Verne showed her his study and wished her luck. He later described Nellie as "the prettiest young girl imaginable" but pronounced her "built for hard work." He added, "I am sure I was delighted to see her; and so, too, was Madame Verne, who has never ceased speaking of her since."

From Amiens, Nellie went to Calais, France, where she caught a mail train to Brindisi, Italy. She reached Brindisi in time to board the steamer *Victoria*. It would take her across the Mediterranean Sea, through the Suez Canal, and past the Arabian Peninsula to the port of Colombo, Ceylon (now Sri Lanka), just south of India. Although Nellie took notes throughout her journey, her editors in New York heard little from her. She sent cables when the ship docked and mailed back written reports when she was able. But the cables simply announced her arrival at a new port, and the mail took weeks to reach New York. Nellie's readers back home would have to wait until she returned to learn the whole story of her adventure. In the meantime, the editors of the *World* fanned interest in the voyage by challenging readers to predict the exact length of Nellie's trip in days, hours, minutes, and seconds. The paper printed an entry form every day and promised the winner an all-expenses-paid trip to Europe.

Nellie experienced her first real delay in Colombo. The *Victoria* actually arrived in port two days early, but the *Oriental*, which would take Nellie on the next leg of her trip, had to wait five days to receive passengers from another ship. She passed the time at the Grand Oriental Hotel, where she learned to love the spicy local curry dishes served at the restaurant. Nellie also did her share of sightseeing, but she was more than ready when the *Oriental* set sail on December 13.

"I found it a great relief to be again on the sweet, blue sea, out of sight of land," she wrote. Over the next two weeks, the ship stopped in Penang, on the coast of Malaysia, followed by Singapore, and finally, Hong Kong. By then Nellie had a new traveling companion. While in Singapore, she purchased one of the few souvenirs she would collect on her trip—a monkey. Nellie would name him McGinty and bring him back to New York, where he would make his presence felt in his new home by smashing all the dishes in her kitchen.

After five days in Hong Kong, Nellie and McGinty boarded the *Oceanic* for Yokohama, Japan, arriving on January 2. Nellie was impressed with Japan. She found the country beautiful and declared that its citizens were "the cleanliest people on earth." But the ship had a five-day layover, and Nellie was impatient to sail for San Francisco. By then even the crew of the *Oceanic* was caught up in the race

While waiting for the mail train to leave Calais, France (background), Nellie visited the lighthouse and had something to eat, but her layover was only about two hours. In Hong Kong (inset), Nellie had five days to explore the city and its surroundings.

FRANK LESLIE'S I

FATHER TIME OUTDONE

Even Imagination's Record Pales Bef the Performance of "The World's" lobe-Circler.

NELLIE BLY.

More than 280,300 people bought copies of the January 26, 1890, edition of the *World* (background), which announced the completion of Nellie's record-breaking trip. During the journey, *Frank Leslie's Illustrated Newspaper,* a weekly publication, included this engraving of the famous traveler.

HEN TIME AYS., 6 HRS., 11 MIN., — S

Themselves Hoar

at Nellie Bly's Arrival.

WELCOME SALUTES IN NEW YORK AND BROOK

Vhole Country Aglow with Intense thuslasm.

NELLI BLY TELLS HER STO

A Multitudinous Ovation for the Plucky Traveller at "The World" — The History of Journalism Cannot Parallel This Popular Achievement — "The World's" Editorial Rooms a Bower of Congratulatory Bouquets — Disappointment of a Would-Be Rival — "The World" and Its Representatives Know No Such Word as "Fail."—Next!!!

"Never having failed, I could not picture what failure meant, but I did tell the officers of the Oceanic . . . that I would rather go into New York successful and dead than alive and behind time."

Globe-Circlers at the Remarkable Achievement of "Traveller.

ly and THE WORLD." M. de Lesseps was of o same opinion about the impropriet young girl travelling alone.

WHAT MR. JULES S THINKS.
I called on Jules S ews, and asked his opin of Miss Bly's journey. "Alas!" he answered. "I cannot e enthusiastic about ng the world too small. I I reflection that was nce immense and the admiration of peoples into a little thing to hold in the pa nd. I can well remember the rs ago, when it took myself and three mpanions three days and two night avel from Brest to Paris by diligence. S ourney takes to-day just fifteen hours! he tour around the world was formerly e work of ten years, but nowadays it is e fashionable amusement of rich people. ormerly great men's sons, having finished air education, made a grand tour of the orld slowly. Now they travel faster, th, however, less profit. I cannot ap rove of racing round the world, because

ALL EUROPE ENTHUSIASTIC
Congratulations from Geographers, Scientists and Friends.

[*New York World.*]

SPECIAL CABLE DISPATCH TO WORLD evening papers here and throughout England printed the news that Miss Bly had urg at midnight, and would arrive in New ork this after Germany, and the plucky American girl's success is now known throughout the length and breadth of Europe. Here in England the trip excited an unusual amount of interest, particularly, perhaps, because at the outset the papers had predicted that Miss Bly would not succeed. But they paragraphed her various stages along the journey, and all give her credit now for her

CHEERS FROM JULES VERNE.
He Cables that He Never Doubted the Success of "The World's" Traveller.

tive which whirled her thither. M and strain against each other is a c fierce as if it were for life and de are knocked off, eyeglasses to deliver their famous passenger on time. In her honor, the ship's chief engineer posted a verse on the engine, with the date he hoped to reach California: "For Nellie Bly, We'll win or die. January 20, 1890."

Once she set foot on American soil—on January 21—the excitement about Nellie's adventure seemed to reach a fever pitch. There was some drama as well. A blizzard had halted all train travel through the northern United States, threatening to derail Nellie's race against time. So the *World* arranged for a special train to take her to Chicago via the southern route. In Chicago she transferred to a regular train, which required passengers to get off to eat their meals at various stations along the way. At each stop, Nellie was greeted by crowds of admirers who shook her hand, presented her with flowers, and pressed their faces against restaurant windows to get a glimpse of the famous globetrotter.

Finally, at 3:51 p.m. on Saturday, January 25, 1890, Nellie stepped onto the platform of the train station at Jersey City, New Jersey, marking the end of her journey around the world. She had circled the globe in 72 days, 6 hours, 11 minutes, and 14 seconds, more than seven days faster than Jules Verne's Phileas Fogg. Ever the journalist, Nellie had spent the last legs of her journey composing the account of her adventure that would appear in the *World* the next day. With the lead headline, "Father Time Outdone," the newspaper would devote more than four pages of its January 26 issue to Nellie's trip. Among the many columns of coverage was a short article reporting that Elizabeth Bisland was heading for New York on the *Bothnia,* "one of the slowest ships of the Cunard line," which was "wallowing in the trough of the yeasty Atlantic." Although she failed to beat Nellie, the paper added, Miss Bisland was not forgotten, and the staff of the *World* wished her well.

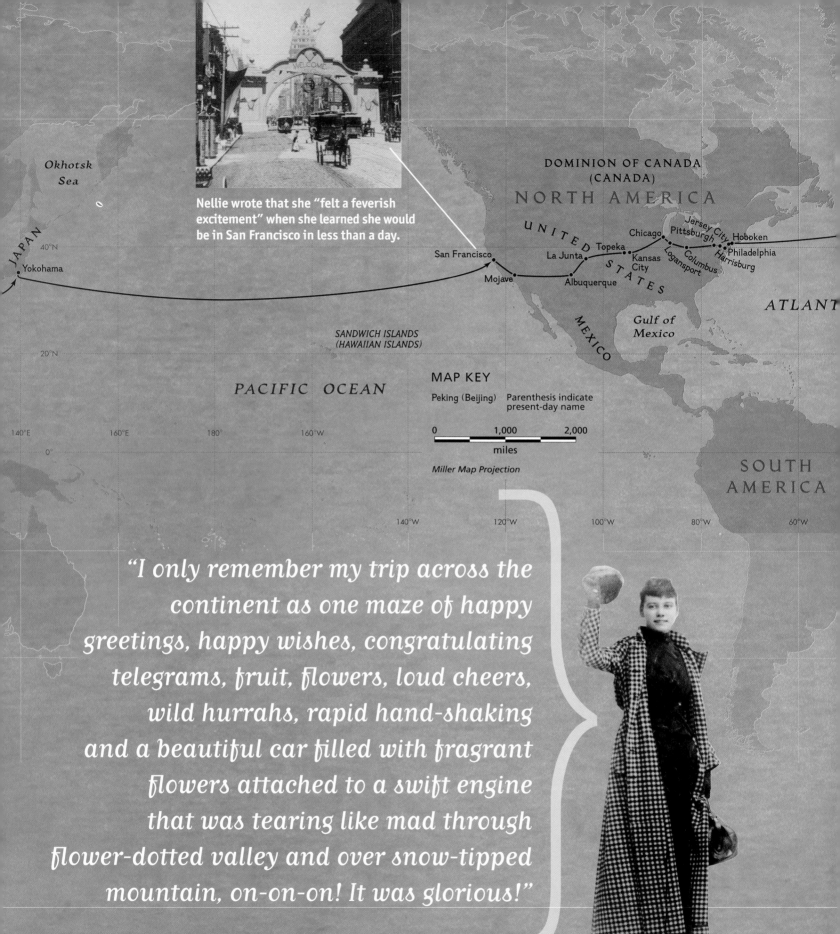

Okhotsk
Sea

JAPAN

Yokohama

40°N

20°N

140°E   160°E   180°   160°W

0°

Nellie wrote that she "felt a feverish
excitement" when she learned she would
be in San Francisco in less than a day.

DOMINION OF CANADA
(CANADA)

NORTH AMERICA

UNITED

San Francisco

Mojave

Chicago

La Junta   Topeka

Albuquerque

Kansas
City

STATES

MEXICO

Jersey City
Pittsburgh   Hoboken

Logansport   Columbus   Philadelphia
Harrisburg

ATLANT

Gulf of
Mexico

SANDWICH ISLANDS
(HAWAIIAN ISLANDS)

PACIFIC   OCEAN

MAP KEY

Peking (Beijing)   Parenthesis indicate
present-day name

0   1,000   2,000
miles

Miller Map Projection

SOUTH
AMERICA

140°W   120°W   100°W   80°W   60°W

"I only remember my trip across the
continent as one maze of happy
greetings, happy wishes, congratulating
telegrams, fruit, flowers, loud cheers,
wild hurrahs, rapid hand-shaking
and a beautiful car filled with fragrant
flowers attached to a swift engine
that was tearing like mad through
flower-dotted valley and over snow-tipped
mountain, on-on-on! It was glorious!"

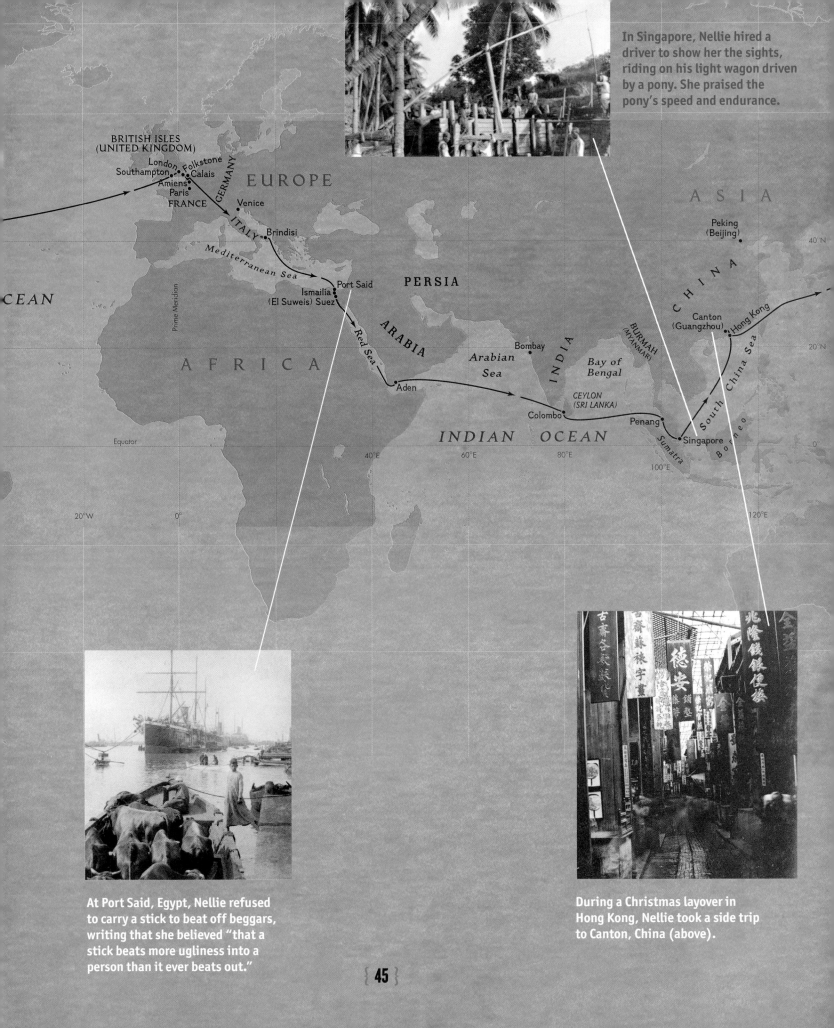

In Singapore, Nellie hired a driver to show her the sights, riding on his light wagon driven by a pony. She praised the pony's speed and endurance.

OCEAN

BRITISH ISLES
(UNITED KINGDOM)

London Folkstone
Southampton   Calais
Amiens
Paris
FRANCE

GERMANY

EUROPE

ASIA

Venice

ITALY

Brindisi

Mediterranean Sea

Prime Meridian

Port Said

Ismailia
(El Suweis) Suez

PERSIA

Peking
(Beijing)

CHINA

Canton
(Guangzhou)

Hong Kong

Red Sea

ARABIA

AFRICA

Aden

Bombay

INDIA

Arabian
Sea

Bay of
Bengal

BURMAH
(MYANMAR)

South China Sea

CEYLON
(SRI LANKA)

Colombo

Penang

Sumatra

Singapore

Borneo

INDIAN OCEAN

Equator

40°E   60°E   80°E   100°E

40°N

20°N

120°E

20°W   0°

At Port Said, Egypt, Nellie refused to carry a stick to beat off beggars, writing that she believed "that a stick beats more ugliness into a person than it ever beats out."

{ 45 }

During a Christmas layover in Hong Kong, Nellie took a side trip to Canton, China (above).

On February 8, 1890, *Frank Leslie's Illustrated Newspaper* commemorated Nellie's trip around the world with these engravings. They show Nellie receiving a "golden globe" (top left), her arrival in Philadelphia (bottom right), and her reception in Jersey City at the completion of her journey (center).

A more detailed account of Nellie's journey ran in the *World* during the month of February, and the winner of the "Nellie Bly Guessing Match" was revealed. F. W. Stevens of New York City beat out close to one million other entrants by predicting Nellie's travel time within two-fifths of a second. Meanwhile, Nellie found herself to be quite a celebrity. Advertisers used her exploits to sell cakes, clothing, canned goods, and other products. McLoughlin Brothers issued a board game that followed the day-by-day progress of her trip. She also went on a lecture tour and compiled all of her globetrotting reports into *Nellie Bly's Book: Around the World in Seventy-two Days*. But while the public embraced Nellie, her editors at the *World* failed to reward her with a bonus or a raise. Feeling insulted and angry, Nellie left Pulitzer's paper to pursue other opportunities.

Nellie Bly's famous byline was absent from New York's daily newspapers for more than three years. But it could be found in the *New York Family Story Paper*, a weekly magazine. Nellie signed a three-year contract for an impressive sum of $40,000 to provide that publication with serials, or ongoing fiction stories. With only her imagination to fall back on and no experience developing plots or characters, it was a difficult assignment. Still, Nellie had high hopes for this foray into fiction. "You know all the great English novelists began in this way," she wrote to her friend in Pittsburgh, Erasmus Wilson. "So I feel encouraged."

Just seven months later, Nellie sent Wilson another letter that was decidedly less upbeat. Her brother Charles had died in 1890 at age 28, and Nellie had been helping to care for his wife and two young children. She also had taken ill herself, and that brought on a long bout of depression. "I suddenly became a victim of the most frightful depression that ever beset [a] mortal," Nellie wrote in a letter in March 1891. "You can imagine how severe it is when I tell you that I have not done a stroke of work for four weeks." After months of feeling poorly, Nellie sought a change of scenery in Europe. She finally

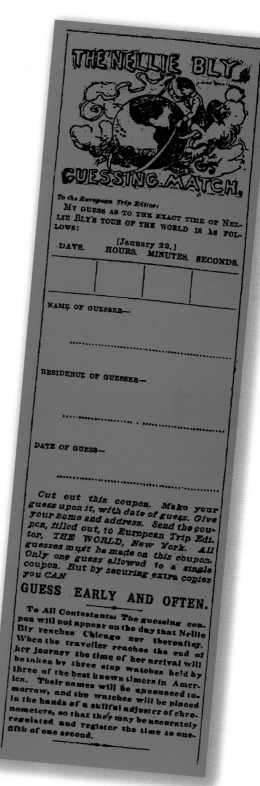

Thanks to Nellie's trip and the daily entry forms for the "Nellie Bly Guessing Match," the *World's* circulation grew steadily throughout December 1889 and January 1890.

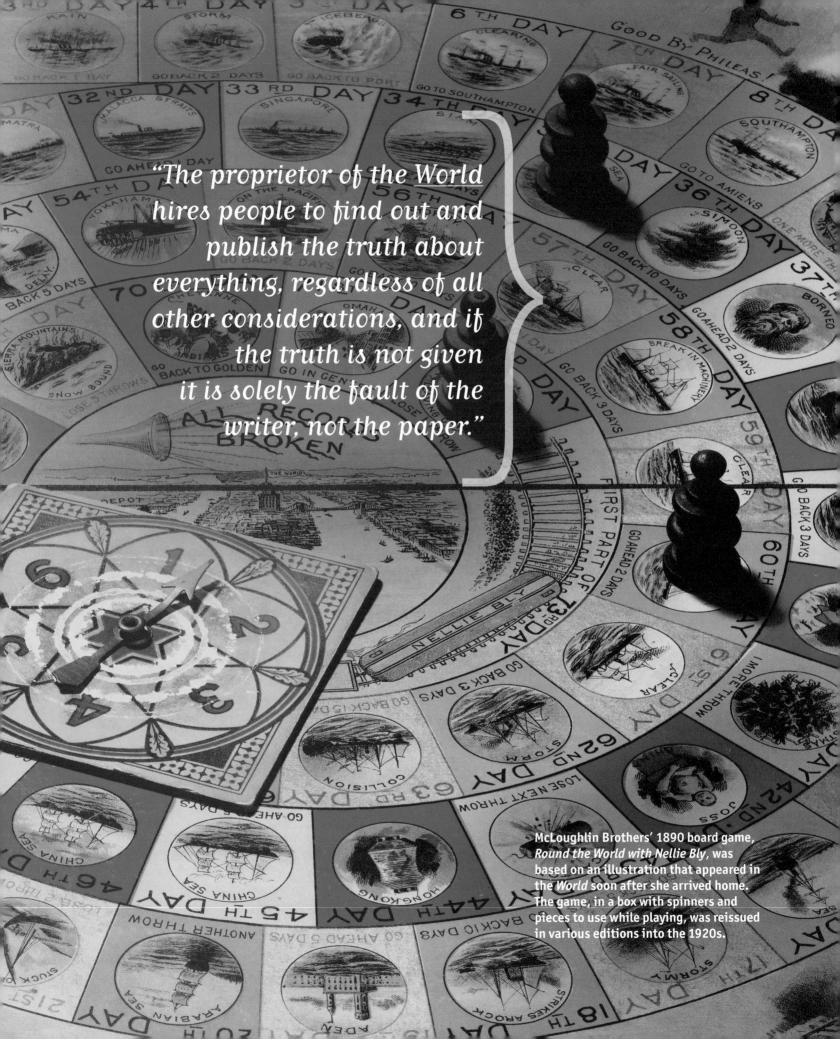

"The proprietor of the _World_ hires people to find out and publish the truth about everything, regardless of all other considerations, and if the truth is not given it is solely the fault of the writer, not the paper."

McLoughlin Brothers' 1890 board game, _Round the World with Nellie Bly_, was based on an illustration that appeared in the _World_ soon after she arrived home. The game, in a box with spinners and pieces to use while playing, was reissued in various editions into the 1920s.

rejoined the high-pressure world of journalism in 1893, when the *World*'s new editor asked if she might be interested in coming back. On September 17, the *World* welcomed her first article since 1890 with the headline "Nellie Bly Again."

By now Nellie was a seasoned reporter, and she contributed a wide variety of articles to the *World*. She investigated a triple murder, delved into police corruption, and interviewed Emma Goldman, the radical activist who was in jail on charges of inciting a riot. In 1894, she traveled to Chicago, Illinois, to cover the violent strike of railroad workers against the Pullman Palace Car Company. Instead of focusing only on the issues behind the strike or the violence that had erupted, Nellie started by talking to the strikers and their families in the company town of Pullman. She went on to interview the governor of Illinois, as well as Eugene V. Debs, leader of the union that had called for the strike.

Nellie's work in Illinois impressed the editors of some local newspapers, and in February 1895, she was offered a job on the *Chicago Times-Herald*. Ready for something new, she took it.

Nellie interviewed two of her most famous subjects in jail. In September 1893 she introduced her readers to Emma Goldman (top), whom she called "an unusual and extraordinary woman." In January 1895, she profiled American Railway Union leader Eugene V. Debs (bottom), who was serving a six-month sentence for his actions during the Pullman Strike.

When he met Nellie, Robert Livingston Seaman was a successful businessman, having made his fortune running a wholesale grocery company. In 1869, he started the Iron Clad Manufacturing Company to make cans for shipping milk on railroad trains. An article announcing his marriage to Nellie called Seaman "one of the most carefully dressed men in New York."

But the job was short-lived. After only five weeks, she quit the paper and made an even bigger change in her life. On April 5, 1895, Nellie Bly, age 30, married Robert Livingston Seaman, a 70-year-old millionaire from New York whom she had met at a dinner only two weeks before. Nellie's friends and family were shocked. Seaman's loved ones were suspicious. They were sure that Nellie had married the confirmed bachelor for his money. The marriage was such a surprise that one magazine wondered if it was another example of stunt reporting, in which Nellie would pretend to be married and then write about the experience. Regardless of the public's curiosity, Nellie never addressed the issue of her marriage in print. It was one of the few aspects of her life that she kept private.

While Nellie would write a number of articles for the *World* in 1896—including a very personal interview with women's rights advocate Susan B. Anthony—her marriage was the start of a new stage in her life. She and her husband spent three years in Europe, returning in 1899 so he could take care of problems at his business, the Iron Clad Manufacturing Company. Before too long, Nellie also became intimately involved in the workings of the company, which made milk cans, boilers, automobile gas tanks, garbage cans, and other products. She started in November

After her marriage, Nellie moved into her husband's home on West 37th Street in New York City, and also enjoyed his weekend house in upstate New York. "Few young women have had more worldly experience at the age of 30 than Miss Bly," wrote the *World,* "and few are more capable of enjoying the pleasures of a 'millionaire existence.'"

In her February 2, 1896, article on Susan B. Anthony, Nellie wrote, "Susan Anthony is all that is best and noblest in woman. She is ideal, and if we will have in women who vote what we have in her, let us all help to promote the cause of woman suffrage."

1899, as a way to cope with the death of her sister, Kate, at age 32. But it was another death that made the Iron Clad Nellie's responsibility. On February 6, 1904, Robert Seaman was hit by a horse and wagon while crossing the street. On March 11, 1904, he died of heart disease brought on by his injuries. Not yet 40 years old, Elizabeth Cochrane Seaman was now a widow.

After her husband's death, Nellie solidified her position as president and owner of the Iron Clad. As a reporter, she had interviewed workers and managers in a number of different industries, and she used what she had learned to create a modern, employee-friendly company. The Iron Clad's headquarters in Brooklyn, New York, had a gym with showers, a dining room, a library, and even a small hospital. The 1,500 employees received guaranteed weekly salaries, rather than being paid piece by piece for the items they made. Mrs. Seaman "maintains that it is the duty of every employer of labor, whether he employs one or 10,000, to do what he can to make their lives happier and brighter," the Iron Clad's general manager told the *Brooklyn Daily Eagle* in 1905. Unfortunately, Nellie paid far less attention to the business details of the company. By 1909, it became clear that something was wrong with the Iron

Clad's finances. Despite having a thriving factory and many customers, the company always seemed to be short of money.

In fact, several employees in the finance department had been working together in a long and complicated scheme to steal money from the Iron Clad. In the end, they stole close to $2 million and plunged Nellie into court cases that continued for years. Besides the trial of the two former employees at the heart of the crime, there was Nellie's fight against her creditors, the people and companies to whom the Iron Clad owed money. Her employees' crimes had left the company unable to pay its bills, so the creditors sought relief where they could find it. After selling off what was left of the Iron Clad to raise money, the court also sold a house that Nellie owned. The creditors then sought to take over another business Nellie had started, the American Steel Barrel

Nellie's metal business card for the 1901 Pan-American Exposition in Buffalo, New York, declares her unique position in the business world on the front and shows the Iron Clad's factory on the back. Background: a 1906 ad for Iron Clad Steel Shipping and Storage Barrels.

Company, but the court wouldn't allow it. Instead, Nellie paid $50,000 to settle the Iron Clad's remaining debts.

Nellie watched the final stages of this drama from a distance. On August 1, 1914, she left New York for a three-week vacation in Austria. She ended up staying close to five years. Four days before she set sail, Austria had declared war on Serbia in the beginning of the Great War, or World War I. Suddenly Nellie's trip was more than just a chance to escape her troubles. Once in Austria, her instincts as a journalist took over and she campaigned hard for the chance to report from the front lines. In late October, she was one of four foreigners— and the only woman—allowed to visit the war zone. She spent a month writing about what she saw at the Russian and Serbian fronts, sending back articles that were published in the *New York Evening Journal*.

During her stay in Europe, Nellie developed a great affection for the Austrian people. After the war was over, she urged U.S. officials to help rebuild the country's economy. But when she returned to New York in February 1919, her focus shifted to her own survival. Nellie had left all her money and property with her elderly mother for safekeeping, but her mother had given everything to Nellie's brother, Albert. He also had taken over the Steel Barrel Company. Nellie and Albert had feuded for years, and now he refused to return anything to her. "I struggled all my life to gain comfort and independence for my mother," she wrote to Erasmus Wilson in March 1919, "and that mother deserts me and crushes me." Nellie took Albert to court to try and get her business back. Until matters with him were settled, however, she needed to make a living.

In May 1919, Nellie started writing regularly for the *New York Evening Journal*,

When she visited the war zone, Nellie, shown here with an Austrian officer (top), sent back vivid reports. "One after the other six shells fell and buried themselves in the same soft earth," she wrote in the *New York Evening Journal* on December 8, 1914. "Then I got into the trench.... I was not afraid. I would not run. Yet my mind was busy. I thought another shot would follow. It will doubtless be better aimed. If it does, we shall die. And if so, what then?"

After returning home safely in 1919, Nellie (bottom, right) used the power of her pen to find help for a young widow who was having difficulty taking care of her two children.

covering such diverse topics as boxer Jack Dempsey's heavyweight championship fight and the gruesome confession of a teenaged murderer. She also answered letters from readers in a column on the editorial page, giving advice on marriage, motherhood, and other topics. Often, Nellie shared her opinions on issues of the day. She wrote against gambling, for birth control, and against capital punishment. More and more, she used her column to change people's lives. She found jobs for needy mothers and helped abandoned children find homes.

In her late 50s, Nellie was as active and adventurous as she had been when

As she grew older, Nellie, shown here in 1921, returned to the career that made her famous. Her last article appeared in the *New York Evening Journal* just 18 days before she died.

"I have never written a word that did not come from my heart. I never shall. I have never had but one desire, and that was to benefit humanity."

she was a young, globetrotting reporter. But the years started to catch up with her. Throughout 1920 and 1921 she suffered from bronchitis, characterized by coughing and breathing problems. Not one to pamper herself, she continued working at a furious pace, skipping meals and ignoring the medications that were prescribed for her. Finally, on January 9, 1922, she entered St. Mark's Hospital in New York with pneumonia, a lung disease. That same day, the *New York Evening Journal* ran the last article Nellie would ever write. It was a thoughtful column on fate. "Is it possible for us to struggle and overcome fate," Nellie asked, "or are we merely being swept along a course which all our efforts fail to alter or change?"

Nellie died at 8:35 a.m. on January 27, 1922. The following day, the *Evening Journal* carried a tribute by Arthur Brisbane, her boss and longtime friend. "Nellie Bly was THE BEST REPORTER IN AMERICA," wrote Brisbane, "and that is saying a good deal. . . . She takes with her from this earth all that she cared for, an honorable name, the respect and affection of her fellow workers, the memory of good fights well fought and of many good deeds never to be forgotten by those that had no friend but Nellie Bly. Happy the man or woman that can leave as good a record."

Afterword

At a time when many women lived unassuming lives, Nellie Bly made people sit up and take notice. If she wasn't making history herself, she was writing about others who did. The story of the two decades before and after the turn of the 20th century was her story, and she shared it through her powerful pen. She profiled leaders, exposed corruption, and offered her readers a travelogue that expanded their horizons even as it made the world a little smaller.

Rarely does anyone leave a more detailed record of her place in the world than Nellie Bly. Hers was a public life. She shared her feelings and opinions through her writing and embraced the struggles of all classes of Americans who were fighting for their rights. Her words live on even now, inviting anyone who's interested to read her articles and explore her version of America during a time of great growth and social change.

Yet for many years, Nellie was virtually forgotten. Her grave had no headstone, and the few attempts to capture her strength and passion in popular culture fell short. In 1946, a musical comedy titled *Nellie Bly* opened on Broadway to negative notices and closed after only 16 performances. A 1981 TV movie, *The Adventures of Nellie Bly*, also received lackluster reviews. Perhaps the most fitting tribute in the mass media came on a 2000 episode of *The West Wing*, in which

After five decades of neglect, Nellie's grave at Woodlawn Cemetery in the Bronx, New York, is now adorned with fresh flowers and a U.S. flag. Among the other celebrities buried at the cemetery are jazz great Duke Ellington, feminist Elizabeth Cady Stanton, and Nellie's boss at the *World*, Joseph Pulitzer.

fictional first lady Abbey Bartlet goes to Cochran's Mills to dedicate a statue of Nellie. When it becomes clear that President Jed Bartlet doesn't know who Nellie was, Abbey proceeds to educate him.

In the real world, Nellie's legacy was rescued by her fellow writers. In 1978, the New York Press Club erected an elegant memorial stone at her gravesite at Woodlawn Cemetery in the Bronx, New York. Every year, that same group recognizes Nellie's accomplishments at a young age with the Nellie Bly Cub Reporter Award. It is given to the best journalistic effort by a reporter who has been in the business less than three years.

Author's Note

In July 1995, the Apollo Area Historical Society dedicated this Pennsylvania state historical marker in front of Nellie's first home in Apollo.

NELLIE BLY
(1864-1922)

A crusading journalist on Pittsburgh and New York newspapers, she won fame for her daring exploits and her investigations of social ills. In 1889-90, Bly circled the globe in 72 days. She was born Elizabeth Cochran and lived here as a child.

PENNSYLVANIA HISTORICAL AND MUSEUM COMMISSION 1995

Nellie Bly didn't have the benefit of a tape recorder when she interviewed subjects for her newspaper articles. Nor did she take many notes, particularly when she was undercover on one of her "stunt" assignments. How, then, did Nellie manage to report the detailed quotations and dialogue that filled her articles? Either she had a phenomenal memory or, more likely, she reconstructed quotes and events as accurately as her memory would allow.

Today, journalistic standards are tougher. Since reporters have the technology to capture interviews directly, most newspaper editors expect them to quote exactly what was said. Reporters sometimes fix grammatical mistakes, a practice that many editors and interview subjects think is acceptable. But journalists who depend on their memories to reconstruct quotes or who make up quotes altogether have been known to lose their jobs. Times definitely have changed since the 1890s.

Chronology

May 5, 1864 Elizabeth Jane Cochran is born in Cochran's Mills, Pennsylvania

July 19, 1870 Father dies

1879 Spends one term at the State Normal School in Indiana, Pennsylvania. Adds an "e" to the end of last name.

1880 Moves with family to Pittsburgh

January 25, 1885 Writes first published article for the *Pittsburg Dispatch*

February 1, 1885 Uses byline Nellie Bly for first time

1886 Travels to Mexico to write articles for the *Pittsburg Dispatch*

1887 Moves to New York City

August 21, 1887 The *Pittsburgh Dispatch* publishes her article on women journalists

October 9, 1887 Her two-part exposé on life at the Women's Lunatic Asylum on Blackwell's Island begins in the *New York World*

November 14, 1889 Leaves on trip around the world

January 25, 1890 Completes trip around the world in 72 days, 6 hours, 11 minutes, and 14 seconds

February 1895 Takes job at the *Chicago Times-Herald*. Quits after five weeks.

April 5, 1895 Marries Robert Livingston Seaman in Chicago

November 1899 Starts working at the Iron Clad Manufacturing Company

March 11, 1904 Robert Seaman dies of heart disease

1909 First suspects wrongdoing at the Iron Clad

August 1, 1914 Leaves New York for Austria four days after war begins in Europe

December 4, 1914 The *New York Evening Journal* publishes her first report from the war front

February 28, 1919 Returns to New York from Europe

May 1919 Begins writing regularly for the *New York Evening Journal*

January 9, 1922 The *New York Evening Journal* publishes her last column

January 27, 1922 Dies of pneumonia in New York City

In September 2002, the U.S. Postal Service issued "Women in Journalism" stamps to commemorate the work of four pioneering female reporters. Besides Nellie, the 37-cent stamps honored war correspondent Marguerite Higgins, investigative journalist Ida Tarbell, and the "first lady of the black press," Ethel Payne.

Resources

BOOKS

Bausum, Ann. *Muckrakers*. Washington, DC: National Geographic Society, 2007.

A generation after Nellie Bly started writing exposés, Ida Tarbell, Lincoln Steffens, and Upton Sinclair took up the call. This compelling book looks at the contributions these journalists and others have made to investigative journalism.

Kroeger, Brooke. *Nellie Bly: Daredevil, Reporter, Feminist*. New York: Times Books, 1994.

This comprehensive volume is the authoritative source on Nellie's life and work, dense with facts and references and yet a joy to read. In the absence of a Nellie Bly archive, it is the most satisfying resource for excerpts of Nellie's writing and the details of her story.

Verne, Jules. *Around the World in 80 Days*. New York: Penguin Books, 2004. (Originally published in French in 1873.)

On a bet, the wealthy gentleman Phileas Fogg and his servant try to circle the globe in 80 days. This novel was the inspiration for Nellie's feat in 1889–90.

VIDEO

"Around the World in 72 Days," *The American Experience,* PBS Home Video, 1997 (VHS); WGBH Boston, 2006 (DVD).

Brooke Kroeger, author of the authoritative 631-page book on Nellie Bly's life and career, was the principal consultant for this entertaining, educational 1997 documentary, originally shown on PBS.

WEBSITES

Nellie Bly's Book: Around the World in Seventy-two Days. New York: The Pictorial Weeklies Company, 1890.

digital.library.upenn.edu/women/bly/world/world.html

Ten Days in a Mad-House by **Nellie Bly.** New York: Ian L. Munro, Publisher, 1887.

digital.library.upenn.edu/women/bly/madhouse/madhouse.html

Read the complete text of Nellie's books recounting her ten days in the Women's Lunatic Asylum on Blackwell's Island and her trip around the world, available through "A Celebration of Women Writers," a digital archive with more than 300 out-of-print books written by women.

In Seven Stages: A Flying Trip Around the World by Elizabeth Bisland. New York: Harper and Bros., 1891.

erc.lib.umn.edu/dynaweb

Elizabeth Bisland's account of her own trip around the world is available online, thanks to the "Women's Travel Writing Digitization Project" of the University of Minnesota. Search the website above.

The American Experience: Around the World in 72 Days.

www.pbs.org/wgbh/amex/world

This site elaborates on the 1997 PBS documentary about Nellie. It includes an interactive map of her journey around the world, a teacher's guide, and even an audio recording of the Stephen C. Foster song "Nelly Bly."

PLACE TO VISIT

Newseum
555 Pennsylvania Avenue, N.W.
Washington, DC 20001
888-NEWSEUM; newseum.org

At this museum focusing on the news media of yesterday and today, enter the Walter and Leonore Annenberg Theater for a four-dimensional trip through time and space. Among the stops is a visit to Blackwell's Island alongside Nellie Bly. The museum also has one of Nellie's original bags from her trip around the world.

Soon after Nellie traveled around the world faster than Jules Verne's fictional hero, Phileas Fogg, companies produced a series of advertising cards celebrating her feat. The cards, with verses and drawings of Nellie on the front, promoted everything from cakes to cigars on the back.

Sources of Quotes

Here are the sources of all the quotations used in this book. A full citation is given the first time a source is mentioned. After that, the citation is abbreviated.

p. 5 display quote, ("Among the Mad," by Nellie Bly, *Godey's Lady's Book*, January 1889, in *Nellie Bly: Daredevil, Reporter, Feminist* by Brooke Kroeger, New York: Times Books, 1994, p. 85); p. 12 display quote, (*Around the World in Seventy-Two Days,* Chapter XIII: Christmas in Canton); p. 15, "Ford has been generally drunk..." (Kroeger, p. 20); p. 18, "If the writer..." (*Pittsburg Dispatch*, January 17, 1885, in Kroeger, p. 39); p. 19, "shy little girl" (*Pittsburg Commercial Gazette*, January 25, 1890, in Kroeger, p. 39); p. 20, "Let a youth start..." and "Their lives would be brighter" ("The Girl Puzzle," by Orphan Girl (Elizabeth Cochrane), *Pittsburg Dispatch*, January 25, 1885); p. 21, "At first I was very much ashamed..." ("Our Workshop Girls: Pretty Females in the Wireworks," by Nellie Bly, *Pittsburg Dispatch*, February 22, 1885); p. 22 display quote, ("The Girl Puzzle"); p. 23 caption, ("Our Workshop Girls: The Story of a Commonplace Hinge," by Nellie Bly, *Pittsburg Dispatch*, March 1, 1885); p. 24, "If we had more people like Nellie Bly..." (*Pittsburg Dispatch*, October 17, 1885, in Kroeger, p. 55); p. 25, "I defied their gaze..." (*Pittsburg Dispatch*, June 20, 1886, in Kroeger, p. 68); p. 26 display quote, (*Pittsburg Dispatch*, August 1, 1886, in Kroeger, p. 70); p. 27, "the worst monarchy..." (*Pittsburg Dispatch*, August 1, 1886, in Kroeger, p. 70); p. 28, "a lady, ambitious...," "impossible not to exaggerate," "The men do not feel at liberty...," "What they are fitted for is so limited" ("Women Journalists," by Nellie Bly, *Pittsburg Dispatch*, August 21, 1887); p. 30, "I never in my life turned back..." ("Among the Mad," in Kroeger, p. 84); p. 31, "positively demented" and "I consider her a hopeless case..." ("Behind Asylum Bars," by Nellie Bly, *New York World*, October 9, 1887); p. 32 display quote, ("Behind Asylum Bars"); pp. 34-35, "human rat-trap," food descriptions, "this is charity," and "suffering sisters" ("Inside the Madhouse," by Nellie Bly, *New York World*, October 16, 1887); p. 36, "Nothing was too strenuous..." (*This Is the Life!,* by Walt McDougall, New York: Alfred A. Knopf, 1926); p. 37, "The significance of the trip..." ("Miss Bly Plans Her Trip," *New York World*, November 14, 1889); p. 39, "I am not racing..." (*Around the World in Seventy-Two Days,* Chapter XII: British China, by Nellie Bly, New York: The Pictorial Weeklies Company, 1890); p. 40, Jules Verne's comments (*New York World*, December 29, 1889, Kroeger, p. 147); p. 41, "I found it a great relief..." (*Around the World in Seventy-Two Days*, Chapter X: In the Pirate Seas); p. 41, "the cleanest people..." (*Around the World in Seventy-Two Days*, Chapter XV: One Hundred and Twenty Hours in Japan); p. 42 display quote, ("From Jersey Back to Jersey," by Nellie Bly, *New York World*, January 26, 1890); p. 43, "For Nellie Bly..." (*Around the World in Seventy-Two Days*, Chapter XVI: Across the Pacific); p. 43, "one of the slowest ships..." and "wallowing in the trough..." ("The Story of a Tour: How an Ambitious Young Woman Failed to Make a World Record," *New York World*, January 26, 1890); p. 44 caption (top), "felt a feverish excitement" (*Around the World in Seventy-Two Days*, Chapter XVI: Across the Pacific); p. 44 caption (right), "that a stick beats more ugliness..." (*Around the World in Seventy-Two Days*, Chapter VII: Two Beautiful Black Eyes); p. 45 display quote, (*Around the World in Seventy-Two Days*, Chapter XVII: Across the Continent); p. 47, "You know all the great English novelists..." (Letter to Erasmus Wilson, August 22, 1890, quoted in "Forgotten Friendship" by George Swetnam, *Pittsburgh Press*, January 15, 1967); p. 47, "I suddenly became a victim..." (Letter to Erasmus Wilson, March 1891, quoted in "Forgotten Friendship"); p. 48 display quote, (*New York World*, July 17, 1894, in Kroeger, p. 238); p. 49 caption, "an unusual..." ("Nellie Bly Again: She Interviews Emma Goldman and Other Anarchists," *New York World*, September 17, 1893); p. 50 caption, "one of the most carefully dressed..." (*New York World*, April 21, 1895, in Kroeger, p. 267); p. 51 caption, "Few young women..." (*New York World*, April 21, 1895, in Kroeger, p. 264); p. 52 caption, "Susan Anthony is all that is best and noblest in woman. ..." ("Champion of Her Sex," by Nellie Bly, *New York World*, February 2, 1896); p. 52, "maintains that it is the duty..." (*Brooklyn Daily Eagle*, Dec. 3, 1905, in Kroeger, pp. 306-307) ; p. 54, "I struggled all my life..." (Letter to Erasmus Wilson, March 29, 1919, Carnegie Library of Pittsburgh); p. 55 caption, "One after the other..." ("Nellie Bly on the Battlefield," by Nellie Bly, *New York Evening Journal*, December 8, 1914); p. 56 display quote, (*New York Evening Journal*, April 6, 1920, in Kroeger, p. 481); p. 57, "Is it possible..." ("Nellie Bly on Pranks of Destiny," by Nellie Bly, *New York Evening Journal*, January 9, 1922); p. 57, "Nellie Bly was the BEST REPORTER..." ("The Death of Nellie Bly," *New York Evening Journal*, January 28, 1922, in Kroeger, pp. 509-510).

Illustration Credits

Index

Founded in 1888, the National Geographic Society is one of the largest nonprofit scientific and educational organizations in the world. It reaches more than 285 million people worldwide each month through its official journal, NATIONAL GEOGRAPHIC, and its four other magazines; the National Geographic Channel; television documentaries; radio programs; films; books; videos and DVDs; maps; and interactive media. National Geographic has funded more than 8,000 scientific research projects and supports an education program combating geographic illiteracy.

For more information, please call 1-800-NGS LINE (647-5463) or write to the following address:
National Geographic Society
1145 17th Street N.W.
Washington, D.C. 20036-4688 U.S.A.

Visit us online at www.nationalgeographic.com/books.

Librarians and teachers, visit us at www.ngchildrensbooks.org.

Kids and parents, visit us at kids.nationalgeographic.com.

For information about special discounts for bulk purchases, please contact National Geographic Books Special Sales: ngspecsales@ngs.org.

For rights or permissions inquiries, please contact National Geographic Books Subsidiary Rights: ngbookrights@ngs.org.

PRINTED IN CHINA.